Smartypants Quiz Book

BEANObooks
geddes & grosset

**Calling all you Smartypants!
Get your brain in gear and
see how well you do
answering the questions
in this brand new
Smartypants Quiz Book.**

**Each page has 10 questions
- one on each of the
subjects shown on the page
opposite.**

At the end of
each page, jot down
how many correct
answers you get and be
amazed at what a
Smartypants you
are!

SPORT THE WORLD

NUMBERS

ANIMALS

FOOD
AND DRINK

BOOKS
AND FILMS

ODD ONE
OUT

MUSIC

PEOPLE

LUCKY DIP

SPORT

1.
Which game is played with 22 balls, including 15 reds and 1 white?

THE WORLD

2. In which American city would you find the White House?

NUMBERS

3.
How many years are there in a decade?

STAMP!

ANIMALS

4. Does a jaguar have spots or stripes?

FOOD AND DRINK

5. What is the main ingredient of coleslaw?

BOOKS AND FILMS

6.
Which late actor played Professor Dumbledore in the first two Harry Potter films?

ODD ONE OUT

MUSIC

8. What is a lullaby?

7. Which one is it? Sagittarius, Pluto, Jupiter

LUCKY DIP

PEOPLE

9. What does a meteorologist study?

10. When texting, what do the initials BBL stand for?

Answers

1. Snooker 2. Washington. 3. Ten. 4. Spots. 5. Cabbage 6. Richard Harris. 7. Sagittarius. The other two are planets. 8. A song to send babies to sleep. 9. The weather. 10. Back before long.

5

SPORT

1. Which sport uses foils?

THE WORLD

2. Which city is known as The Big Apple?

NUMBERS

3. How many Bash Street Kids are there?

ANIMALS

4. In Australia, which animal is known as a joey?

FOOD AND DRINK

5. In America they are called cookies. What are they called in Britain?

BOOKS AND FILMS

6. Dodie Miller wrote 101 Dalmatians. True or False?

ODD ONE OUT

7. Which one is it? Flute, tuba, drum.

MUSIC

8. Marshall Mathers III is better known by what name?

PEOPLE

9. Name the female presenter of The Saturday Show.

LUCKY DIP

10. What is a cantaloupe?

7

SPORT

1.
Name three sports beginning with the letter "R".

THE WORLD

2. In which ocean would you find The Azores?

NUMBERS

3. What were the numbers on the Mad Hatter's hat in Alice in Wonderland?

FOOD AND DRINK

5. What type of food is ravioli?

ANIMALS

4. What is unusual about a chameleon?

BOOKS AND FILMS

6. In The Princess Diaries, of which country was Mia a Princess?

ODD ONE OUT

7. Which one is it? Windsor, Buckingham or Holyrood

MUSIC

8. Complete the title of this song. Jenny From The -----

PEOPLE

9. Name Sabrina's cat.

LUCKY DIP

10. What is the second colour of a rainbow?

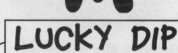

9

SPORT

1. In which country were the very first Olympic Games held?

THE WORLD

2. Which country would you visit to try to find the Loch Ness monster?

NUMBERS

3. What is the missing number? 2, 3, 5, 8, 12 ?

ANIMALS

4. Ragdoll, Burmese and Maine Coon are all breeds of which animal?

FOOD AND DRINK

5. What is the main ingredient of smoothies?

BOOKS AND FILMS

6. Which animals took over Toad's house in The Wind In The Willows?

ODD ONE OUT

7. Which one is it? Wool, silk, nylon

MUSIC

8. Name the lead singer of The Rolling Stones.

PEOPLE

9. The Danes are natives of which country?

LUCKY DIP

10. In which soap will you find Summer Bay?

Answers

1. Ancient Greece. 2. Scotland. 3. 17. 4. Cat. 5. Milk. 6. Weasels. 7. Nylon. The other two are natural fabrics. 8. Mick Jagger. 9. Denmark. 10. Home and Away.

SPORT

1. In which sport would you use a sweeping brush?

THE WORLD

2. The Pyrenees Mountains are between which two countries?

NUMBERS

3. How many players are there in a cricket team?

ANIMALS

4. What animals belong to the bovine category?

FOOD AND DRINK

5. What type of food is asparagus?

BOOKS AND FILMS

6. In which book would you find Tinkerbell?

ODD ONE OUT

7. Which one is it? Panorama, EastEnders, Coronation Street.

MUSIC

8. Which ex-member of Boyzone has appeared in Coronation Street?

PEOPLE

9. Charlotte Church appeared in a film called "I'll Be There!" True or False?

LUCKY DIP

10. What kind of creature is a cassowary?

Answers

1. Curling. 2. France and Spain. 3. Eleven. 4. Cattle 5. A vegetable. 6. Peter Pan. 7. Panorama. The other two are soaps. 8. Keith Duffy. 9. True. 10. Bird.

SPORT

1. With which sport do you associate Michael Jordan?

THE WORLD

2. What name is given to a mountain which erupts and produces lava?

NUMBERS

3. How many are in a score?

ANIMALS

4. What kind of animal is Scooby-Doo?

FOOD AND DRINK

5. If you had a tortilla, would you eat it or drink it?

BOOKS AND FILMS

6. Who wrote the story The Twits?

ODD ONE OUT

7. Which one is it? Blue, orange, green.

MUSIC

8. If you had a clarsach, would you pluck it or blow it?

PEOPLE

9. By what title is a Sultan's wife known?

LUCKY DIP

10. Who is the host of Who Wants to be a Millionaire?

Answers

1. Basketball. 2. A volcano. 3. Twenty. 4. A dog. 5. Eat it! 6. Roald Dahl. 7. Orange (the others are primary colours). 8. Pluck it. 9. Sultana. 10. Chris Tarrant.

SPORT

1. What is the name of the official ensuring fair play in a game of cricket?

THE WORLD

2. Southern Ireland is also known as Eire. True or false?

NUMBERS

3. How many years are there between leap years?

FOOD AND DRINK

5. What dish do the Americans traditionally eat on Thanksgiving Day?

ANIMALS

4. In The Magic Roundabout, what kind of animal is Ermintrude?

BOOKS AND FILMS

6. In Harry Potter and the Philosopher's Stone, what hatched from an egg owned by Hagrid?

ODD ONE OUT

7. Which one is it? Skye, Man, Orkney

MUSIC

8. Jennifer Lopez is also known by what name?

PEOPLE

9. Which Jubilee did the Queen celebrate in 2003?

LUCKY DIP

10. What is bling bling?

Answers

1. Umpire. 2. True. 3. Four. 4. A cow. 5. Roast turkey. 6. A dragon. 7. Man - the other two islands are in Scotland. 8. J-Lo. 9. Golden. 10. Flashy jewellery.

SPORT

1. In which sport would you find a chukker?

THE WORLD

2. Where is St Mark's Square?

NUMBERS

3. How many correctly numbered balls are needed to win the lotto jackpot?

ANIMALS

4. What does a farrier do to horses?

FOOD AND DRINK

5. By what name are French fries also known?

BOOKS AND FILMS

6. How many 'Jurassic Park' films have been made?

ODD ONE OUT

7. Which one is it? Chow, Collie, Persian.

MUSIC

8. Doh, ray, me ... What note comes next?

PEOPLE

9. Who wrote 'The Series Of Unfortunate Events' books?

LUCKY DIP

10. Name Bart Simpson's baby sister.

Answers

1. Polo. 2. Venice. 3. Six. 4. Shoes them. 5. Chips. 6. Three. 7. Persian. The other two are breeds of dog. 8. Fah. 9. Lemony Snicket. 10. Maggie.

SPORT

1. With which sport do you associate Venus and Serena Williams?

THE WORLD

2. Where would you be if you were sailing in a gondola?

NUMBERS

3. How many Harry Potter books are planned?

ANIMALS

4. The Dodo is now extinct. What kind of creature was it?

FOOD AND DRINK

5. Name Desperate Dan's favourite food.

BOOKS AND FILMS

6. Who wrote The Wee Free Men?

ODD ONE OUT

7. Which one is it? Satsuma, lime, apple.

MUSIC

8. Mattie, Charlie and James make up which group?

PEOPLE

9. In which soap would you find Spencer Moon?

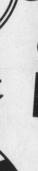

LUCKY DIP

10. David Beckham plays for Barcelona. True or false?

Answers

1. Tennis. 2. Venice. 3. Seven. 4. A bird. 5. Cow pie (giant!). 6. Terry Pratchett. 7. Apple (the other two are citrus fruits). 8. Busted. 9. EastEnders. 10. False. He plays for Real Madrid.

SPORT

1. Fill in the missing letters to find the sport.
-OL- E - -A-L.

THE WORLD

2. Name the capital of Peru.

NUMBERS

3. On which channel is the soap Family Affairs?

ANIMALS

4. In which book is Piglet found?

FOOD AND DRINK

5. Basil, thyme and mint are all types of what?

BOOKS AND FILMS

6. What do the films Chicago and Bridget Jones's Diary have in common?

ODD ONE OUT

7. Which one is it? Dancer, Prancer, Flash.

MUSIC

8. How many people sing in a trio?

PEOPLE

9. What is the name of the Queen of The Netherlands?

LUCKY DIP

10. Coronation Street is set in Weatherfield. True or False?

Answers

1. Volleyball. 2. Lima. 3. Channel 5. 4. Winnie the Pooh. 5. Herbs. 6. Renee Zellweger starred in both. 7. Flash. The other two are Santa's reindeer. 8. Three. 9. Beatrix. 10. True.

SPORT

1. What sport is known as The Sport of Kings?

THE WORLD

2. What is Buddhism?

NUMBERS

3. On the "Seventh day of Christmas" what did my true love send to me?

ANIMALS

4. A Caribou is an American reindeer. True or false?

FOOD AND DRINK

5. What type of food is a Frankfurter?

24

BOOKS AND FILMS

6.
In which book would you find a dog called Nana?

ODD ONE OUT

7.
Which one is it?
Cardiff, Aberdeen, Llandudno.

MUSIC

8. What are sea shanties?

PEOPLE

9.
What is the surname of Mary-Kate and Ashley?

LUCKY DIP

10.
Which British monarch abdicated in 1936?

Answers

1. Horse racing. 2. A religion which has its origins in India. 3. Seven swans a-swimming. 4. True. 5. A small smoked sausage. 6. Peter Pan. 7. Aberdeen. The other two cities are in Wales. 8. Work songs of sailors from long ago. 9. Olsen. 10. Edward VIII.

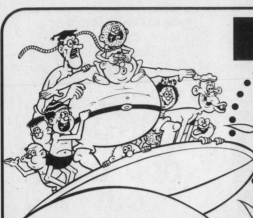

SPORT

1. Which sport can be played on a horse, in water, or on a bicycle?

THE WORLD

2. In which country is EuroDisney?

NUMBERS

3. How many are in a dozen?

FOOD AND DRINK

5. Borsch is a soup. What is it made from?

ANIMALS

4. From which animals do we get mohair?

BOOKS AND FILMS

6. What was the title of the follow up film to Home Alone?

ODD ONE OUT

7. Which one is it? The Archers, Holby City, The Bill.

MUSIC

8. Who sang the song Sk8er Boi?

PEOPLE

9. Ms Dynamite's real name is Niomi. True or False?

LUCKY DIP

10. Name Superman's girlfriend.

Answers

1. Polo. 2. France. 3. Twelve. 4. Goats. 5. Beetroot. 6. Home Alone II — Lost in New York. 7. The Archers. The other two are television programmes. 8. Avril Lavigne. 9. True. 10. Lois Lane.

SPORT

1. On what surface is the game of curling played?

THE WORLD

2. In which country would you find the Arc de Triomphe?

NUMBERS

3. Is 13×8 more or less than 14×7?

ANIMALS

4. Which is larger — an ostrich or an emu?

FOOD AND DRINK

5. What type of food are pecans?

BOOKS AND FILMS

6. Who wrote The Tale of Squirrel Nutkin?

ODD ONE OUT

7. Which one is it? Mozart, Rembrandt, Picasso.

MUSIC

8. Andrea, Caroline, Jim and Sharon are members of which group?

PEOPLE

9. In the tv sitcom Friends, what did Rachel call her baby?

LUCKY DIP

10. Beside which river would you find The London Eye?

Answers

1. Ice. 2. France. 3. More. 4. An ostrich. 5. Nuts. 6. Beatrix Potter. 7. Mozart. The other two are artists. 8. The Corrs. 9. Emma. 10. The Thames.

SPORT

1.
Rearrange these letters to find the name of a sport - TRECICK

THE WORLD

2. What is the capital city of Wales?

NUMBERS

3. How many times did the clock strike in the rhyme Hickory Dickory Dock?

ANIMALS

4. Which creatures were turned into horses to pull Cinderella's coach in the fairy story?

FOOD AND DRINK

5. Which fruit do we associate with tennis at Wimbledon?

BOOKS AND FILMS

6. What colour is Shrek in the film of the same name?

ODD ONE OUT

7. Which one is it? Nevis, Everest, Windermere.

MUSIC

8. What do the letters CD stand for?

PEOPLE

9. What is the name of the Queen's second oldest son?

LUCKY DIP

10. In which fictional London borough is EastEnders set?

Answers

1. Cricket. 2. Cardiff. 3. One. 4. White mice. 5. Strawberries. 6. Green. 7. Windermere. The other two are mountains. 8. Compact Disc. 9. Andrew. 10. Walford.

SPORT

1. In which sport would you find the word deuce?

LITTER

CUTHBERT CRINGEWORTHY

THE WORLD

2. What nationality was Hans Christian Andersen?

NUMBERS

3. What is the highest number on a dice?

FOOD AND DRINK

5. If you were eating in a taverna, which country would you be in?

ANIMALS

4. What is a baby elephant called?

BOOKS AND FILMS

6. Name the author of the Artemis Fowl books.

ODD ONE OUT

7. Which one is it? September, May, April.

MUSIC

8. Rearrange the letters to find the name of a famous boy band — FELWSTEI.

PEOPLE

9. What is the name of Dennis the Menace's pet pig?

LUCKY DIP

10. Who was the male star of the film Moulin Rouge?

33

SPORT

1. Everton football club is from Birmingham. True or false?

THE WORLD

2. All Saints' Day comes after which date?

NUMBERS

3. How many Billy Goats Gruff were there in the fairy story?

FOOD AND DRINK

5. What is the main ingredient of the Indian dish Dahl?

ANIMALS

4. What type of animal is a komodo dragon?

BOOKS AND FILMS

6.
Who plays the character Ebeneezer Scrooge in The Muppets — A Christmas Carol?

ODD ONE OUT

7. Which one is it? Cabbage, peas, beans.

MUSIC

8.
Complete the title of the famous song — "The hills are alive ---- --- ----- -- -----"

PEOPLE

9.
The Dalai Lama was once ruler of which country?

LUCKY DIP

10. Mix together yellow and blue and what colour do you get?

Answers

1. False. They are from Liverpool. 2. Halloween. 3. Three. 4. A lizard. 5. Lentils. 6. Michael Caine. 7. Cabbage. The other two grow in pods. 8. With the sound of music. 9. Tibet. 10. Green.

SPORT

1. What nationality is Tiger Woods?

THE WORLD

2. In which country is Brussels?

NUMBERS

3. What is a group of eight called?

ANIMALS

4. What type of animal was Simba?

FOOD AND DRINK

5. In the Harry Potter books, a well-known type of sweet comes in very unusual flavours. Do you know what it is?

BOOKS AND FILMS

6. Name the leading Bug in the film, 'A Bug's Life'?

ODD ONE OUT

7. Which one is it? Holland, Denmark, Sweden.

MUSIC

8. Complete the title of the film starring Eminem. Eight ----

PEOPLE

9. Which singer lives at a place called Neverland?

LUCKY DIP

10. A marsupial carries its young in a pouch. True or false?

Answers

1. American. 2. Belgium. 3. Octet. 4. A lion. 5. Jelly Beans. 6. Flik.
7. Holland. The other two are Scandinavian countries. 8. Miles.
9. Michael Jackson. 10. True.

SPORT

1. In which sport would you find a steeplechaser?

THE WORLD

2. How many countries share a border with Wales?

NUMBERS

3. How many Ugly Sisters did Cinderella have?

ANIMALS

4. What breed of dog is most commonly used to round up sheep?

FOOD AND DRINK

5. What type of cheese would you normally sprinkle on pasta?

BOOKS AND FILMS

6. Complete the film title — Bend It Like - - - - - - - .

ODD ONE OUT

7. Which one is it? Leeds, Edinburgh, Dublin.

MUSIC

8. What is the name of the famous concert hall in Kensington, London?

PEOPLE

9. What is the name of Barbie's boyfriend?

LUCKY DIP

10. What part of your body gets a manicure?

39

SPORT

1. Which insect and game share the same name?

THE WORLD

2. Which body of water separates England and France?

NUMBERS

3. How many feet has a biped?

PYOING!

ANIMALS

4. If an animal is a herbivore, what does it eat?

FOOD AND DRINK

5. The scientific name for water is H_2O. True or false?

BOOKS AND FILMS

6. Name the young gardener in the book The Secret Garden?

ODD ONE OUT

7. Which one is it? Victoria, Joy, Elizabeth.

MUSIC

8. In music, what does the term fortissimo mean?

PEOPLE

9. David Beckham's younger son has the same name as a Shakespeare character. What is it?

LUCKY DIP

10. Donny Osmond was lead singer of which 70's group?

Answers

1. Cricket. 2. The English Channel. 3. Two. 4. Plants and grasses. 5. True. 6. Dickon. 7. Joy. The other two are the names of British Queens. 8. Very loud. 9. Romeo. 10. The Osmonds.

SPORT

1. Which British city hosted the 2002 European Games?

THE WORLD

2. What is the second tallest mountain in the world?

NUMBERS

3. How many people make up a set of quads?

ANIMALS

4. Which fictional character could 'talk to the animals'?

FOOD AND DRINK

5. Do cucumbers grow above or below the ground?

BOOKS AND FILMS

6. Complete the title of this popular Christmas film. Miracle on ---- ------

ODD ONE OUT

7. Which one is it? Holly, mistletoe, lilac?

MUSIC

8. What is a jingle?

PEOPLE

9. What is the name of the daughter in tv's Absolutely Fabulous?

LUCKY DIP

10. Who wrote Budgie the Helicopter books?

Answers

SPORT

1. In which game do you use hoops and mallets?

THE WORLD

2. What is the capital of the U.S.A.?

NUMBERS

3. How many wise monkeys were there?

ANIMALS

4. What do we call a group of fish?

FOOD AND DRINK

5. What is the main ingredient of porridge?

BOOKS AND FILMS

6. Which superhero did Toby McGuire play?

ODD ONE OUT

7. Which one is it? Paddington, Rupert, Snoopy.

MUSIC

8. In the musical film Bugsy Malone, all the actors are children. True or false?

PEOPLE

9. If someone walks the catwalk, what do they do for a living?

LUCKY DIP

10. What is a pomegranate?

Answers

1. Croquet. 2. Washington. 3. Three. 4. A school. 5. Oatmeal. 6. Spiderman. 7. Snoopy. The other two are bears. 8. True. 9. Model clothes. 10. A fruit.

45

SPORT

1. In which sport would you use a puck?

THE WORLD

2. Which is the world's largest ocean?

NUMBERS

3. If you add a baker's dozen to the number of days in a leap year, what number do you get?

FOOD AND DRINK

5. Pineapples grow on trees. True or false?

ANIMALS

4. Who had a dog called Toto?

BOOKS AND FILMS

6.
Which actor is well known for his line "I'll be back" in The Terminator?

ODD ONE OUT

7. Which one is it? Daisy, dahlia, dandelion.

MUSIC

8. Whose first number one was I Should Be So Lucky?

PEOPLE

9. Who is said to have played the fiddle while Rome burned?

LUCKY DIP

10. What is the currency in Thailand?

Answers

1. Ice hockey. 2. Pacific. 3. 379. 4. Dorothy in The Wizard of Oz.
5. False. 6. Arnold Schwarzenegger. 7. Dahlia - the others
are weeds. 8. Kylie Minogue. 9. Nero. 10. The baht.

47

SPORT

1.
Which football team plays at Highbury?

THE WORLD

2. In which country would you find the Angel Falls?

NUMBERS

3. What is the station platform number in the Harry Potter books?

ANIMALS

4. What is an ostrich's running speed - 20, 30 or 40 miles an hour?

FOOD AND DRINK

5. What kind of fruit is a Granny Smith?

BOOKS AND FILMS

6.
Unscramble these letters to spell a Spielberg film - JUNIJAM.

ODD ONE OUT

7. Which one is it? Octopus, starfish, spider.

MUSIC

8.
Who sang the theme song for the film Titanic?

PEOPLE

9.
Which Shakespearean character fell in love with Juliet?

LUCKY DIP

10.
What's the correct spelling — accidentle, accidental or acidental?

Answers

1. Arsenal. 2. Venezuela. 3. 9%. 4. 40 mph. 5. Apple. 6. Jumanji.
7. Starfish - the others have eight legs.
8. Celine Dion. 9. Romeo.
10. Accidental.

49

SPORT

1. What colour of ball is worth five points in snooker?

THE WORLD

2. Which country reminds you of Christmas dinner?

NUMBERS

3. In the nursery rhyme, how many blackbirds were baked in a pie?

ANIMALS

4. A hippo can run faster than a man. True or false?

FOOD AND DRINK

5. What's the traditional food eaten by Scots on Burns' Night?

BOOKS AND FILMS

6. Who was the ring-bearer in the Lord of the Rings trilogy?

ODD ONE OUT

7. Which is it? Eggs, butter or cheese.

MUSIC

8. What is Madonna's middle name?

PEOPLE

9. Who was the first president of the USA?

LUCKY DIP

10. If you were a campanologist, what would you be doing?

SPORT

1. Which sport would you be playing if you scored a birdie?

THE WORLD

2. What language is spoken in Brazil?

NUMBERS

3. How many sides does a fifty pence piece have?

ANIMALS

4. What's the plural of octopus - octopuses or octopi?

FOOD AND DRINK

5. Which vegetables can be baked or runner?

BOOKS AND FILMS

6.
Name the film in which a pig thought he was a sheepdog.

ODD ONE OUT

7. Which one is it? Thailand, China or Hawaii.

MUSIC

8. Which group did Geri Halliwell belong to before going solo?

PEOPLE

9. Who painted the Mona Lisa?

LUCKY DIP

10. What date is Valentine's Day?

Answers

8. The Spice Girls. 9. Leonardo da Vinci. 10. February 14th.
6. Babe. 7. Hawaii - the others are in the Far East.
1. Golf. 2. Portuguese. 3. Seven. 4. Octopuses. 5. Beans.

SPORT

1. In which sport would you do a Fosbury Flop?

THE WORLD

2. Which city would you be in if you could see The Colisseum?

NUMBERS

3. How many leaves does a lucky clover have?

ANIMALS

4. A Friesian is a breed of which animal?

FOOD AND DRINK

5. Which is the correct spelling - brocolli or broccoli?

BOOKS AND FILMS

6. What kind of dog starred in the film Beethoven?

ODD ONE OUT

7. Which one is it? Cabbage White, Pink Panther or Red Admiral.

MUSIC

8. If you were playing a clarinet, would you blow into it, use drumsticks on it or squeeze it?

PEOPLE

9. Who was the nursery rhyme character who kissed the girls and made them cry?

LUCKY DIP

10. Mel Gibson was born in America. True or false?

Answers

1. High jump. 2. Rome. 3. Four. 4. Cow. 5. Broccoli.
6. St Bernard. 7. Pink Panther - the others are butterflies.
8. Blow into it. 9. Georgie Porgie. 10. False.

55

SPORT

1. What sport do the Dallas Cowboys play?

THE WORLD

2. If you saw a car with the plate NL on it, which country would it be from?

NUMBERS

3. What's the number of the Prime Minister's home in Downing Street?

FOOD AND DRINK

5. Chocolate is made from cocoa beans - true or false?

ANIMALS

4. What was the name of highwayman Dick Turpin's horse?

BOOKS AND FILMS

6. In the film Antz, what was the name of the ant who fell in love with Princess Bala?

ODD ONE OUT

7. Which is it? Garfield, Scooby-Doo or Pluto.

MUSIC

8. Which TV channel shows Top of the Pops?

PEOPLE

9. Who wrote The Little Mermaid?

LUCKY DIP

10. Who chases The Road Runner in the cartoon?

Answers

1. American Football. 2. Netherlands. 3. Ten. 4. Black Bess. 5. True. 6. Z (pronounced Zee). 7. Garfield - the others are dogs. 8. BBC 1. 9. Hans Christian Andersen. 10. Wile E. Coyote.

SPORT

1.
If you were at Centre Court, which sport would you be watching?

THE WORLD

2. In which country is the Grand Canyon?

NUMBERS

3.
Which number is associated with bad luck?

ANIMALS

4.
Flamingos can fly - true or false?

FOOD AND DRINK

5.
What is a crepe?

BOOKS AND FILMS

6.
What do the letters BFG stand for in the title of Roald Dahl's book?

ODD ONE OUT

7. Which one is it? Dollar, dime, dinar.

MUSIC

8.
Robbie Williams was in which boy band before going solo?

PEOPLE

9.
What is the Queen's surname?

LUCKY DIP

10. What do the letters www stand for in computing?

Answers

1. Tennis. 2. America. 3. Thirteen. 4. True. 5. A pancake. 6. Big Friendly Giant. 7. Dinar - the others are American currency. 8. Take That. 9. Windsor. 10. World Wide Web.

SPORT

1. What's the centre of a dartboard called?

THE WORLD

2. Naples is in Italy - true or false?

NUMBERS

3. Finish the title - The ----- Musketeers.

ANIMALS

4. What is unusual about a Manx cat?

FOOD AND DRINK

5. If someone gave you some tikka masala, would you drink it or eat it?

BOOKS AND FILMS

6.
Into which superhero does Clark Kent turn?

MUSIC

8.
Who was the winner of the TV programme Pop Idol in 2002?

ODD ONE OUT

7. Which one is it? Lion, tiger, panther.

LUCKY DIP

10.
What colour are the pieces in a game of chess?

PEOPLE

9. Who lived in the Garden of Eden?

Answers

1. Bull's-eye. 2. True. 3. Three. 4. It has no tail. 5. Eat it. 6. Superman. 7. Tiger - the others don't have stripes. 8. Will Young. 9. Adam and Eve. 10. Black and white.

SPORT

1. How many years are there between Olympic Games?

THE WORLD

2. Heathrow airport is located at which major city?

NUMBERS

3. How many Friends are there in the TV series?

ANIMALS

4. What kind of creatures are kept in an aquarium?

FOOD AND DRINK

5. What do Americans call candy floss?

BOOKS AND FILMS

6. What's the name of the third Harry Potter book?

ODD ONE OUT

7. Which one is it? Ginger beer, coffee, cocoa.

MUSIC

8. Who are the brothers in the band Oasis?

PEOPLE

9. Alexander Graham Bell invented the television. True or false?

LUCKY DIP

10. What time of day is a.m. - before or after noon?

Answers

1. Four. 2. London. 3. Six. 4. Fish and other sea creatures. 5. Cotton candy. 6. The Prisoner of Azkaban. 7. Ginger beer - the others came from beans. 8. Liam and Noel Gallagher. 9. False - he invented the telephone. 10. Before.

SPORT

1.
Which sport is associated with lightweight and featherweight?

THE WORLD

2. Before Euros were introduced, what was the currency of Spain?

NUMBERS

3.
Which number should you dial in an emergency?

ANIMALS

4. Cygnets are the young of which bird?

FOOD AND DRINK

5.
What kind of sandwiches does Paddington Bear eat?

BOOKS AND FILMS

6.
Complete the film title -
Honey, I ------ The Kids.

ODD ONE OUT

7. Which one is it? August, winter, spring.

MUSIC

8. Which instrument does Vanessa Mae play?

PEOPLE

9. A native of Australia is called an Aborigine. True or false?

LUCKY DIP

10. What is Shrove Tuesday also known as?

Answers

SPORT

1. How long does the first half of a football match last?

THE WORLD

2. Where in Britain would you see the Angel of the North?

NUMBERS

3. What do you call an ice cream cornet with a chocolate flake in it?

ANIMALS

4. Does a puffin have feathers or fins?

FOOD AND DRINK

5. What is a pistachio - a pastry or a nut?

BOOKS AND FILMS

6. Charles Dickens wrote Oliver Twist. True or false?

ODD ONE OUT

7. Which one is it? Hurricane, flood, gale.

MUSIC

8. Which former pop band had a number one hit with the Bee Gees' song, Tragedy?

PEOPLE

9. What is the name of David Beckham's wife?

LUCKY DIP

10. If your hobby was philately what would you collect?

SPORT

1. Would you use a racket or a bat to play baseball?

THE WORLD

2. Which island is bigger - Majorca or Iceland?

NUMBERS

3. How many sides does a dice have?

ANIMALS

4. Which is the first animal listed in the dictionary?

FOOD AND DRINK

5. Is Edinburgh Rock soft or hard?

BOOKS AND FILMS

6. What do the letters PG beside a film title stand for?

ODD ONE OUT

7. Which one is it? Pisces, Neptune, Virgo.

MUSIC

8. Where does Avril Lavigne come from - Australia or Canada?

PEOPLE

9. Which Scottish leader was played by Mel Gibson in the film Braveheart?

LUCKY DIP

10. Complete the collective noun - a ------ of whales

Answers

1. A bat. 2. Iceland. 3. Six. 4. Aardvark. 5. Soft. 6. Parental Guidance. 7. Neptune - the others are signs of the zodiac. 8. Canada. 9. William Wallace. 10. School.

SPORT

1.
The same letter is missing from these three sports. Find it to complete the words.
G - L F ; P -L- ; JUD-

THE WORLD

2. In which country was The Lord of The Rings filmed?

NUMBERS

3.
In imperial weights, what does the symbol lb stand for?

ANIMALS

4. Standard, Miniature, French. What breed of dog do these refer to?

FOOD AND DRINK

5.
In Alice in Wonderland, during which meal did the Dormouse sleep?

BOOKS AND FILMS

Complete the following book title — The Chronicles of ......

ODD ONE OUT

7. Which one is it? Rose, Daffodil, Snowdrop.

MUSIC

8. Rearrange the letters to discover a well known male singer. OONB

PEOPLE

9. Of which country was Nelson Mandela president?

LUCKY DIP

10. Jennifer Aniston is married to Johnny Depp. True or False?

SPORT

1.
Name three sports in which you use a bat?

THE WORLD

2. The Palace of Versailles is outside which city?

NUMBERS

3. How many wives did Henry VIII have?

ANIMALS

4.
What type of animal is a hog?

FOOD AND DRINK

5. What is the main ingredient of risotto?

BOOKS AND FILMS

6.
What did the Grinch steal?

ODD ONE OUT

7. Which one is it? Popeye, Homer, Bart.

MUSIC

8.
Who had a hit with the song Let Me Entertain You?

PEOPLE

9.
A Maori is a native of which country?

LUCKY DIP

10.
The Serpentine is the name of a lake in London. True or false?

Answers

73

SPORT

1. Unscramble the letters to find a swimming stroke — LYFUBTETR.

THE WORLD

2. What colours are on the English flag?

NUMBERS

3. How many bears did Goldilocks meet?

ANIMALS

4. Name an Australian animal which carries its young on its back.

FOOD AND DRINK

5. What is a croissant?

BOOKS AND FILMS

6. What type of a book is an annual?

ODD ONE OUT

7. Which one is it? Pork, bacon, steak.

MUSIC

8. How many people sing a duet?

PEOPLE

9. What was the name of Tom Sawyer's friend in Uncle Tom's Cabin?

LUCKY DIP

10. What is the name of the butler in Thunderbirds?

Answers

1. Butterfly. 2. White with a red cross. 3. Three. 4. A koala bear. 5. A crescent-shaped French roll. 6. One which comes out yearly. 7. Steak. The other two are meat from a pig. 8. Two. 9. Huckleberry Finn. 10. Parker.

SPORT

1.
Sir Steven Redgrave is famous for what sport ?

THE WORLD

2. If you were in Grand Central Station, in which city would you be?

NUMBERS

3. How many commandments did Moses receive?

ANIMALS

4. Which animal represents the star sign Aries?

FOOD AND DRINK

5. What is candy floss made from?

BOOKS AND FILMS

6.
The film Hook is based on which story?

ODD ONE OUT

7. Which one is it? Slippy, Happy, Grumpy.

MUSIC

8.
Who became known as Pop Idol's Mr Nasty?

PEOPLE

9.
Which ex-Beatle is the voice of Thomas the Tank engine?

LUCKY DIP

10. Rearrange the letters to find a Pokemon character – UCHIPKA.

Answers

1. Rowing. 2. New York. 3. Ten. 4. The Ram. 5. Spun sugar.
6. Peter Pan. 7. Slippy. The other two are from The Seven Dwarfs.
8. Simon Cowell. 9. Ringo Starr. 10. Pikachu.

SPORT

1. In which sport are Dan levels awarded?

THE WORLD

2. Which is nearer to Britain — America or South Africa?

NUMBERS

3. If something is quadrupled, how many times is it multiplied?

ANIMALS

4. What is an adult leveret called?

FOOD AND DRINK

5. What is soy sauce made from?

BOOKS AND FILMS

6.
What type of creature was Stuart Little?

ODD ONE OUT

7. Which one is it? Waterloo, Waverley, Paddington.

MUSIC

8.
Rearrange the letters to find the name of a popular song by David Gray. NOYBABL

PEOPLE

9.
Name a British country which has sheriffs.

LUCKY DIP

10.
In the pantomime, what is the name of Widow Twankey's son?

Answers

SPORT

1. Wembley Stadium is being replaced with what?

NUMBERS

3. What is the speed limit on British motorways?

THE WORLD

2. What do the initials UN stand for?

ANIMALS

4. Horses are measured in hands. True or false?

FOOD AND DRINK

5. From which fruit is cider made?

BOOKS AND FILMS

6. By what other name is Bruce Banner known?

ODD ONE OUT

7. Which one is it? The Times, The Beano, The Dandy.

MUSIC

8. Who is in charge of an orchestra?

PEOPLE

9. With which sport is Sven Goran Eriksson associated?

LUCKY DIP

10. What are clogs?

Answers

1. A new Wembley Stadium! 2. United Nations. 3. 70 miles per hour. 4. True. 5. Apples. 6. The Incredible Hulk. 7. The Times. The other two are comics. 8. The conductor. 9. Football. 10. Wooden shoes.

SPORT

1. How many pins have to be knocked down in tenpin bowling to make a strike?

THE WORLD

2. What is the biggest animal alive in the world today?

NUMBERS

3. If a person is a centenarian, how old are they?

ANIMALS

4. In the insect world, what are drones?

FOOD AND DRINK

5. What type of food are nectarines?

BOOKS AND FILMS

6.
Who wrote The Selfish Giant?

ODD ONE OUT

7. Which one is it? Pixie, scarecrow, goblin.

MUSIC

8. Who is known as The Princess of Pop?

PEOPLE

9. What is the name of Dennis the Menace's softie enemy?

LUCKY DIP

10. What would you do with a spatula?

Answers

1. Ten! 2. Blue Whale. 3. One hundred. 4. Male of the honey bee. 5. Fruit. 6. Oscar Wilde. 7. Scarecrow. The other two are fairies. 8. Britney Spears. 9. Walter. 10. Spread food with it!

83

SPORT

1. Name three sports which end with the words 'ball?'

THE WORLD

2. Is Mexico north or south of the USA?

NUMBERS

3. The Magi is another name for The Three Wise Men. True or false?

ANIMALS

4. What type of animal is a Jack Russell?

FOOD AND DRINK

5. What are meringues made from?

BOOKS AND FILMS

6.
On which famous outlaw was the film 'The Prince of Thieves' based?

ODD ONE OUT

7.
Which one is it? Primrose, Lily of the Valley, Snowdrop.

MUSIC

8. Which instrument has a coin in its name?

PEOPLE

9.
Genghis Khan was the leader of which ancient people?

LUCKY DIP

10.
In which British country would you find Holyrood Palace?

Answers

1. Football, baseball, basketball, softball and volleyball are five. 2. South. 3. True. 4. A dog. 5. Egg whites and sugar. 6. Robin Hood. 7. Primrose. The other two are white. 8. Penny whistle. 9. The Mongol tribe. 10. Scotland.

SPORT

1. What sport did Pele play?

THE WORLD

2. In which continent is Britain?

NUMBERS

3. How many colours are in the rainbow?

FOOD AND DRINK

5. With which country do you traditionally associate pasta?

ANIMALS

4. Name the dog in the musical Annie.

BOOKS AND FILMS

6. What type of dancer did the film character Billy Elliot become?

ODD ONE OUT

7. Which one is it? Hip-hop, Bling-bling, Rap.

MUSIC

8. Rearrange the letters to find the name of a well-known musical film? ASGREE.

PEOPLE

9. Which actor do you associate with Mr Bean and Blackadder?

LUCKY DIP

10. Who was the puppet whose nose grew when he told a lie?

Answers

SPORT

1.
The All Blacks are a well-known New Zealand cricket team. True or false?

THE WORLD

2. In what country would you find a kookaburra?

NUMBERS

3. Into how many continents is the world divided?

ANIMALS

4. What is a possum short for?

FOOD AND DRINK

5. Where did sushi originate?

BOOKS AND FILMS

6.
Complete the vowels to find one of the cinema's all-time heroes -ND--N- J-N-S

ODD ONE OUT

7. Which one is it? Lion, turtle, crocodile.

MUSIC

8. What do the initials MTV stand for?

PEOPLE

9. Which comedian is known as The Big Yin?

LUCKY DIP

10. What colour is the planet Mars?

Answers

SPORT

1. A shuttlecock is used in the game of badminton. True or false?

THE WORLD

2. If you were at the Eiffel Tower which city would you be in?

NUMBERS

3. What's the missing number? 7, 9, ?, 13.

ANIMALS

4. What kind of animal is a Lhasa Apso?

FOOD AND DRINK

5. Which crop would you find in a paddy field?

BOOKS AND FILMS

6.
What is the name of Batman's car?

ODD ONE OUT

7. Which one is it? Trifle, cheesecake, liquorice allsorts.

MUSIC

8.
Ronan Keating used to sing with Boyzone. True or false?

PEOPLE

9.
Who lives in the White House?

LUCKY DIP

10.
Was a Viking ship known as a tallship or a longship?

SPORT

1.
Frank Bruno
was a famous
English wrestler.
True or false?

NUMBERS

3. In Britain,
how old must
you be to
drive a car?

THE WORLD

2.
In which
country would
you see The
Sphinx?

FOOD AND DRINK

5.
What's
lemon curd –
a spread or a
pudding?

ANIMALS

4. What
animal is the
zodiac sign
of Leo?

BOOKS AND FILMS

6. Complete the film title - The ----- Trousers.

ODD ONE OUT

7. Which one is it? Barn, cottage, mansion.

MUSIC

8. Who sang the theme song from The Lion King?

PEOPLE

9. What is the surname of Harry Potter's friend, Hermione?

LUCKY DIP

10. Name Ozzy Osbourne's youngest son.

Answers

1. False. 2. Egypt. 3. Seventeen. 4. Lion. 5. A spread. 6. Wrong. 7. Barn - the others are houses. 8. Sir Elton John. 9. Grainger. 10. Jack.

SPORT

1. Which sport is played at Cardiff Arms Park?

THE WORLD

2. Name the capital of Austria?

NUMBERS

3. How many people can ride a tandem bike?

ANIMALS

4. Springer, Cocker and King Charles are all breeds of which dog?

FOOD AND DRINK

5. If you were drinking an espresso, what kind of drink would it be?

BOOKS AND FILMS

6. In the Harry Potter books, what is the Dursleys' address?

ODD ONE OUT

7. Which one is it? London, Paris, Milan.

MUSIC

8. Which type of animal did the Pied Piper lead out of Hamelin?

PEOPLE

9. Napoleon was Emperor of which country?

LUCKY DIP

10. Who is the voice of the donkey in Shrek?

Answers

1. Rugby. 2. Vienna. 3. Two. 4. Spaniel. 5. Coffee. 6. 4 Privet Drive. 7. Milan (The others are capital cities). 8. Rats. 9. France. 10. Eddie Murphy.

Well, how did you score?

0–4 – waken up!

5–7 – pretty impressive!

8–10 – who's a real smartypants then?